Basketball's MVPs

READING POWER

KOBE BRYANT

Dan Osier

PowerKiDS press.

New York

Published in 2011 by The Rosen Publishing Group, Inc.
29 East 21st Street, New York, NY 10010

First Edition

Editor: Amelie von Zumbusch
Book Design: Kate Laczynski

Photo Credits: Cover, p. 1 Jeff Gross/Getty Images; p. 4 Jonathan Ferrey/Stringer/Getty Images; pp. 7, 18–19, 22 Andrew D. Bernstein/NBAE/Getty Images; pp. 8–9 Melissa Majchrzak/NBAE/Getty Images; pp. 10–11 John W. McDonough/Getty Images; p. 12 Jed Jacobsohn/Getty Images; p. 15 Todd Warshaw/Getty Images; p. 16 Hector Mata/AFP/Getty Images; pp. 20–21 Gary Bassing/NBAE/Getty Images.

Library of Congress Cataloging-in-Publication Data

Osier, Dan.
  Kobe Bryant / by Dan Osier. — 1st ed.
      p. cm. — (Basketball's MVPs)
  Includes index.
  ISBN 978-1-4488-2523-3 (library binding) —
  ISBN 978-1-4488-2630-8 (pbk.) — ISBN 978-1-4488-2631-5
  (6-pack)
  1. Bryant, Kobe, 1978- 2. Basketball players—United States—Biography. 3. Los Angeles Lakers (Basketball team) I. Title.
  GV884.B794O75 2011b
  796.323092—dc22
  [B]
                          2010021371

Manufactured in the United States of America

CPSIA Compliance Information: Batch #WW11PK: For Further Information contact Rosen Publishing, New York, New York at 1-800-237-9932

CONTENTS

Meet Kobe Bryant 5

The Lakers 6

Kobe Bryant's Life 13

Books................................ 23

Web Sites........................... 23

Glossary............................. 24

Index 24

Kobe Bryant is a basketball player. He was named after a kind of beef from Japan.

Bryant plays for the Los Angeles Lakers. He is a **shooting guard**.

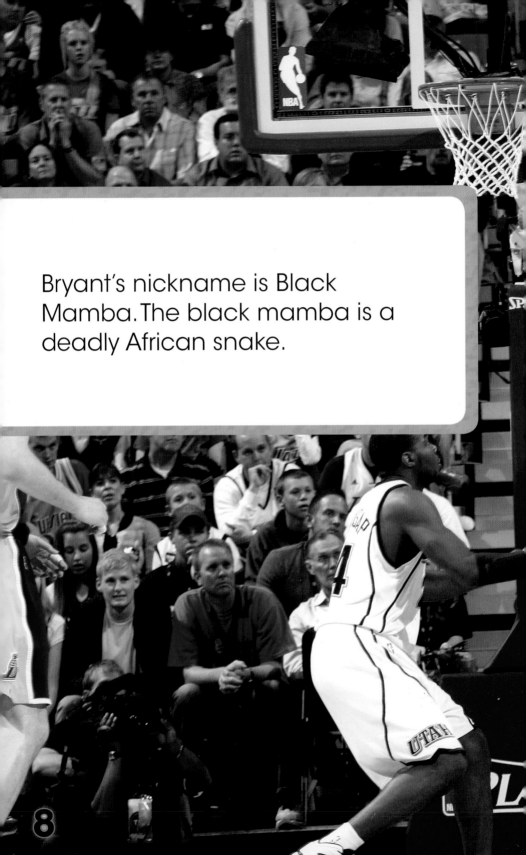

Bryant's nickname is Black Mamba. The black mamba is a deadly African snake.

The Lakers have many great players. Bryant is their biggest star, though.

Bryant was born on August 23, 1978, in Philadelphia, Pennsylvania.

In 1996, Bryant started playing for the Lakers. He was just 18!

15

Bryant helped the Lakers win **championships** in 2000, 2001, and 2002.

In 2008, Bryant was named the NBA's most **valuable** player, or MVP.

In 2009 and 2010, he helped the Lakers win two more championships.

21

Bryant is a great player. He has many **fans**!

BOOKS

Here are more books to read about Kobe Bryant and basketball:

Frisch, Aaron. *Los Angeles Lakers*. NBA Champions. Mankato, MN: Creative Education, 2008.

Pyle, Lydia. *Kobe Bryant*. Awesome Athletes Set III. Edina, MN: Checkerboard Books, 2003.

WEB SITES

Due to the changing nature of Internet links, PowerKids Press has developed an online list of Web sites related to the subject of this book. This site is updated regularly. Please use this link to access the list:
www.powerkidslinks.com/bmvp/kobebry/

GLOSSARY

championships (CHAM-pee-un-ships) Games played to decide the best, or the winner.

fans (FANZ) People who like a well-known person.

shooting guard (SHOO-ting GAHRD) A basketball player whose job is to score points.

valuable (VAL-yoo-bul) Important.

INDEX

C
championship(s),
    17, 21

F
fans, 22

G
game, 8

L
Los Angeles Lakers,
    6, 10, 14, 17, 21

M
MVP, 18

P
Philadelphia,
    Pennsylvania, 13
player(s), 5, 10, 22
points, 8

S
shooting guard, 6